Blaz

UFOs
- are they real?

by David Orme

Ransom

Trailblazers

UFOs - are they real?
by David Orme
Educational consultant: Helen Bird

Illustrated by Elisa Huber and Cyber Media (India) Ltd.

Published by Ransom Publishing Ltd.
Rose Cottage, Howe Hill, Watlington, Oxon. OX49 5HB
www.ransom.co.uk

ISBN   184167 423 0
         978 184167 423 X
First published in 2006

Copyright © 2006 Ransom Publishing Ltd.

Illustrations copyright © 2006 Elisa Huber and Ransom Publishing Ltd.

Additional images courtesy NASA Jet Propulsion Laboratory, NASA Dryden Flight Research Center, NASA/JPL-Caltech, FEMA.

Photograph of Silbury Hill crop circle courtesy (and copyright) Steve Alexander. Visit his website at www.temporarytemples.co.uk to find out more about crop circles, crop circle year books and DVDs.

Every effort has been made to locate all copyright holders of material used in this book. If any errors or omissions have occurred, corrections will be made in future editions of this book.

A CIP catalogue record of this book is available from the British Library.

The rights of David Orme to be identified as the author and of Elisa Huber and Cyber Media (India) Ltd. to be identified as the illustrators of this Work have been asserted by them in accordance with sections 77 and 78 of the Copyright, Design and Patents Act 1988.

Printed in China through Colorcraft Ltd., Hong Kong.

UFOs – are they real?

Contents

UFOs
- are they real?

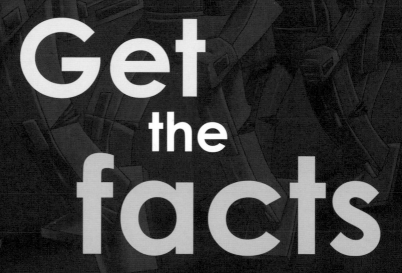

Get
the
facts

Are UFOs real?

UFO means **Unidentified Flying Object**.

It might be:

A weather balloon

A plane

A shooting star

even the Moon.

Or it could be . . . .

An alien space ship.

Many people have
seen UFOs

It's too fast
to be a
plane!

What's
that?

pilots

radar operators

Wow!

Look at that
light in the
sky!

people in a street

fire fighters

Can all these people
be wrong?

What do you think?

Have aliens visited the Earth?

Some people say that they have met aliens.

Some people say they have flown in space ships.

Do you believe them?

Why would people make up stories like this?

Some people say that aliens crashed on the Earth in 1946.

It happened in Roswell, America.

They say that the government kept it secret. They didn't want people to panic.

There are photographs of alien bodies from Roswell.

Are they real or are they fakes?

UFOs from the air

Many pilots have seen UFOs.

Sometimes they are air force pilots.

Radar operators see UFOs on their screens.

Planes are sent up to find them.

The pilots sometimes see objects that move and turn too fast to be planes.

Sometimes pilots see UFOs, but they don't tell anyone.

Why do you think they do this?

A puzzle solved?

Many people said that they saw a strange UFO.

It had lights in a triangle shape. It moved very fast.

Lots of people saw it, but no-one knew what it was.

Now we know about the secret stealth bomber. This is a triangle shape.

The American Air Force was testing it in secret.

Could this be the UFO people saw?

What happens on the ground

People have seen UFOs when they are driving their cars.

Sometimes their engine stops working when the UFO is near.

American soldiers say they saw a UFO land near Rendlesham in England.

Some people didn't believe them. But radiation was found there.

Crop Circles

Sometimes people find strange circles made in crops.

Sometimes they are amazing patterns.

What made the patterns?
People?
The wind?

Or were they made by UFOs?

What do aliens look like?

Are aliens:

Big slimy blobs?   **Giant ants?**

**Like us, only
with blue skin?**

Robots?

People who say they have seen aliens
say they have grey skin and big heads and eyes.

These aliens are sometimes called Greys.

Is this what aliens look like?

There are lots of drawings of Greys, but no one has taken a picture of one.

Some people say:

> *"If everyone who sees an alien say it looks like this, it shows it must be true."*

Other people say:

> *"People say they look like this because they have seen pictures of them."*

What do *you* think?

Alien abduction

Have you been abducted by an alien?

Abducted means taken away from your home. Some people say this has happened to them.

Sometimes the aliens are friendly. They take people for a ride in their UFO.

Sometimes the aliens are unfriendly. They do experiments on people!

There are
stories about
aliens abducting
animals as well as
people.

In America, people say that UFOs have abducted
cows. The cow is pulled up into the UFO using a
ray.

The people say that they have seen the bodies
of the cows after they were abducted.

They say that this is proof
that it happened.

Do you believe this?
What else could
have killed the
cow?

Why might
people
make up
stories
about being
abducted?

17

The Valley of the Zombies

Chapter 1:
A hard climb

Rod and Omar were on holiday in the mountains. They had walked for miles.

"Where are we, Rod?"asked Omar.

Rod pointed to the map.

"Just here. When we get to the top of the path, we will be able to look down into the next valley."

It was hard work climbing the path. At last they got there. They looked down into the valley.

"Look at that!"

Rod and Omar stared down into the valley.

It was amazing. They had never seen anything like it.

At the bottom of the valley there was something big and round. It shone in the sun. It could only be one thing.

A flying saucer!

Chapter 2:
The blue men

There were people walking around. They looked human, but their skin was blue. They wore strange clothes.

Omar had a mobile phone that could take pictures.

"Aliens from space!" said Omar. "Let's go further down. I must get a picture of this!"

They didn't want to be seen. They crept down the valley. They hid behind the rocks.

At last they were near the saucer. Omar stood up to take the picture.

"Oh no you don't!"

Someone had grabbed them from behind.

It was two of the blue men. One of them took Omar's mobile away.

"They speak English!" said Rod.

"Of course we do. We are English!"

"Well, why are you blue then?"

"It's not what you think!"

One of the men rubbed at his face. The blue came off!

Chapter 3:
It's not what you think

"It's just make-up! We are actors. They are making a film here. But they don't want any pictures before the film come out."

The two men seemed quite friendly. They gave Omar his mobile back. He promised not to take any pictures.

"We are having a break at the moment," said one of the men. "Would you like to see inside the flying saucer?"

"That would be great!"

The saucer looked real. It looked strong enough to fly!

They went up some steps into the saucer.

Inside were two aliens. They were like giant, slimy blobs. They each had one eye and a big red mouth. Slime came out of their mouths.

Chapter 4:
The slimy blobs

The aliens were in the saucer control room. There were lots of controls. There were radar screens. It looked very real.

"These aliens are amazing!" said Rod. They look just like real ones!"

Just then the door of the saucer banged shut.

"They are real ones," said one of the men.

Rod and Omar turned around. The two men were holding guns. They fired darts at Omar and Rod. They fell on to the floor.

Then one of the slimy aliens spoke.

"You have done well," it said. "Put the blue make-up on them before they wake up."

The two men bowed and carried Rod and Omar out.

Then the other alien spoke, in its own language.

"Two more zombies to work for us! Taking over this planet is going to be easier than I thought!"

UFO word check

abducted
actors
air force
amazing
America
aliens
banged
believe
bodies
bowed
break
control
drawings
engine
England
English
experiments
fakes
flying saucer
friendly
government
grabbed
holiday
killed
language
mobile phone

mountains
object
panic
patterns
picture
pilot
policemen
proof
radar operators
radar screens
radiation
ray
robots
rubbed
shooting star
slimy
soldiers
stealth bomber
strong
triangle
unfriendly
unidentified
walking
weather balloon
valley
zombies